MW00789514

THE TEEN MINDFULNESS
WORKBOOK

THE TEEN
MINDFULNESS
WORKBOOK

100+ JOURNAL PROMPTS
TO ENCOURAGE GRATITUDE, EASE ANXIETY,
AND INCREASE SELF-ESTEEM

PAPER MOUNTAIN
PUBLISHING

Copyright © 2023 by Paper Mountain Publishing LLC, Pflugerville, Texas

All rights reserved.

No part of this publication may be reproduced, stored in a retrieval system, or transmitted in any form or by any means, electronic, mechanical, photocopying, recording, or otherwise, except as permitted under Sections 107 or 108 of the 1976 United States Copyright Act, without the prior written permission of the Publisher. Requests to the Publisher for permission should be addressed to hello@papermountainpub.com.

Limit of Liability/Disclaimer of Warranty: This publication is sold with the understanding that neither the author nor the publisher is engaged in rendering legal, investment, accounting or other professional services. While the publisher and author have used their best efforts in preparing this book, they make no representations or warranties with respect to the accuracy or completeness of the contents of this book and specifically disclaim any implied warranties of merchantability or fitness for a particular purpose. No warranty may be created or extended by sales representatives or written sales materials. The advice and strategies contained herein may not be suitable for your situation. You should consult with a professional when appropriate. Neither the publisher nor the author shall be liable for any loss of profit or any other commercial damages, including but not limited to special, incidental, consequential, personal, or other damages.

For general information on our products and services, please email hello@papermountainpub.com.

Paper Mountain Publishing LLC publishes its books in a variety of electric and print formats. Some content that appears in print may not be available in electronic books, and vice versa.

TRADEMARKS: Paper Mountain Publishing and the Paper Mountain Publishing logo are trademarks or registered trademarks in the United States and other countries, and may not be used without written permission.

Cover and interior design: TypeJar Studio, LLC

All illustrations used under license from iStock or Adobe Stock.

ISBN: Print 979-8-9885502-0-4

First edition 2023

TABLE OF CONTENTS

"What you are is what you have been. What you'll be is what you do right now."

— *Buddha*

THIS JOURNAL
BELONGS TO:

_____

INTRODUCTION

Hey, Friend! Chances are, this book found its way to you because you are experiencing one of the most exciting yet ever-changing periods of your life: (drumroll, please...)

...YOUR TEENAGE YEARS.

Every...single...adult wishes they had done something differently during these years.

"I wish I had cared less what people thought of me and trusted myself to live boldly."

"I wish I had been a better friend to myself and a better friend to the people in my life."

"I wish I had spent more time in the moment than worrying about the past or the future."

"I wish I had found a way to deal with new challenges and setbacks in healthier ways."

Wow... let's face it: you've got things going on at home, at school, with friends, online, in your body, in the world, over the river, and through the woods. It's easy to get overwhelmed and lose focus (ooh, shiny thing!) when there are endless notifications and deadlines that seem to never end. Don't even get us started on self-esteem, social networks, dating, and how we're supposed to look, feel, and act. Right?

But don't freak out! There is good news: Journaling helps.

Think of how you currently deal with the things that stress you out, causing anxious feelings (enter a big bag of chips and doom-scrolling on Instagram). You might shut down, make impulsive decisions, treat people unkindly or [insert your own behaviors here]. But mindful journaling can be an effective way to help you cope and learn new ways of thinking to manage those stressful and anxiety-inducing situations.

Also, journaling has been shown to improve your memory (win!) and help you find feel-good ways to process your emotions. You will likely benefit from improved relationships (yes, even with your younger sibling) and gain much-needed insight into who you are and what you care about.

Lastly, journaling can shed light on any negative feelings that you have had for a long time. And it can help you spot problems that might need professional guidance. It's important to note that sometimes professional mental health services should be considered if you aren't satisfied with the tools or exercises in this workbook or other self-care resources.

HOW TO USE THIS JOURNAL

First off, why is mindfulness important while journaling?

Mindfulness is being aware of your thoughts, feelings, and actions in each moment. When you experience moments with a mindful eye, you learn to observe situations objectively, build patience, process your feelings, control your reactions and plan for the outcome that you desire. With this awareness, you can develop skills that help you reduce anxious thoughts and feelings. Friend, you might even find that you have learned to react to situations more calmly, with gratitude, and with self-love. Sounds mushy, but it can work.

Gratitude and self-love are two aspects of mindfulness that can profoundly affect your journaling experience.

Gratitude is simply being thankful for the things, opportunities, people, and experiences you have. Some people find that satisfaction and self-esteem can increase when they focus on what they are grateful for. You gotta love yourself, too! Self-love provides the same benefit: When you learn to love and appreciate yourself unconditionally, you can help increase your happiness and self-worth.

Okay, I'm ready to get started. How is this journal organized?

There are four chapters in this book.

Check this out, Friend! Each chapter explores an area of your life that has its own set of challenges: Your home life (I AM LOVED), your education (I AM SMART), your social life (I AM WORTHY), and your self (I AM PERFECT). Each chapter section dives into 5 values that can contribute to a calmer and happier you. The journal has four types of prompts (depending on what you need and how long you have to write), so you can practice incorporating each value within the chapter. Variety is key, and these prompts are meant to fit your needs and schedule.

5-minute quick fix: These prompts offer fast, easy questions to quickly get you in the right mindset when you're short on time.

10-minute reset: These prompts work best when you have a moment before you have to do something you're anxious or worried about.

15-minute regroup: These prompts are designed to reflect or gain insight on things that have happened or will happen.

30-minute deep dive: These prompts allow for longer planning sessions and skills development.

Hop around this journal — it's not meant to be used chapter by chapter. Find the subject you need, and go straight there. If your workload at school is too much for you to handle one week, dive into Chapter 2: I AM SMART. Or if you find yourself stressed out about something going on at home, then spend time journaling in CHAPTER 1: I AM LOVED. This journal is a resource you can keep coming back to whenever you need it.

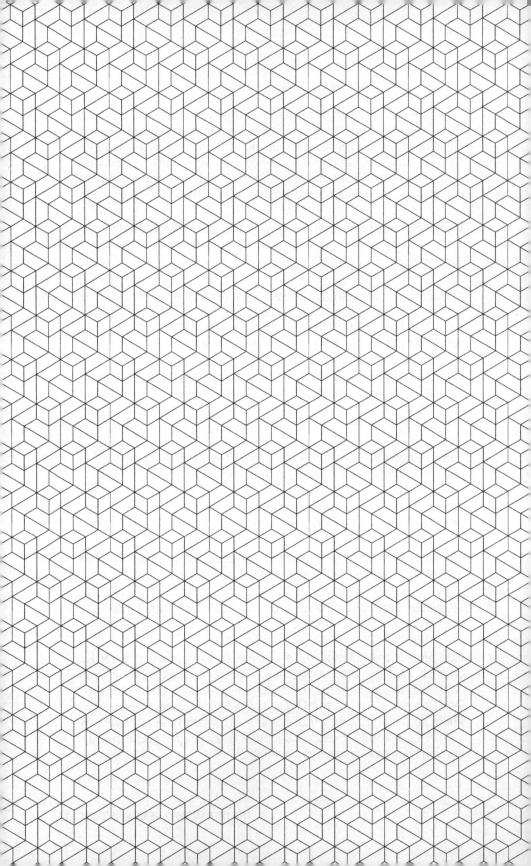

CHAPTER 1: I AM LOVED

Well, Friend, as a teenager, there is no doubt you spend an enormous time at home with your family. (Are you rolling your eyes or smiling right now?) There's no one formula to a family — they're made up of all characters — moms, dads, grandparents, single mom, single dad, double mom, double dad, siblings, no siblings, animals...well, you get it...(Can we please just have a little space??) But, your family is your first introduction to how relationships can give meaning to your life. There's a reason they say, "Home is where the heart is," "There's no place like home," and "Home is a shelter from storms." Home is supposed to be your safe haven from a world of Kardashians and keyboard cats, so let's get to work making that happen.

In this chapter, we'll explore these five values, which can lead to a more calm and peaceful experience at home. (It's possible!)

Respect: Asking for and giving respect to your family, your belongings, and yourself can increase self-esteem and help prevent misunderstandings. You gotta give R-E-S-P-E-C-T, but don't forget to receive it, too.

Trust: Building trust between family members can increase feelings of belonging and safety.

Advocate: Communicating your feelings can help your family understand your needs to make you feel heard, increasing your self-esteem. Friend, it is important to express yourself.

Empathize: Putting yourself in someone else's shoes can help you become more understanding and less reactive in difficult situations.

Contribute: Helping around the house and with your loved ones can give you a sense of responsibility and ownership to keep your space happy and healthy.

Exploring these values can help you create a home environment where you give love and support to your family while also feeling loved and supported in return. Home should be the last place you want to feel stressed out or inadequate.

"We don't need to share the same opinions as others, but we need to be respectful."

— *Taylor Swift, American singer-songwriter*

RESPECT

One of the easiest ways to brighten someone's day in your household is to show them respect and kindness. (And that works both ways! You'll be happier if your family shows you those things, too.)

The way you respond to your parents when they ask you to clean your toothpaste out of the sink, the way your face reacts when your siblings ask you for the millionth time to play a game, the words that come out of your mouth when you're angry, your ability to make eye contact when a family member wants you to listen, knowing that a family member needs help without them having to ask...Friend, these daily exchanges between you guys really add up to create the atmosphere of your home.

Check the vibe, Friend. When you feel like the atmosphere is off (think: way too many disagreements or unkind exchanges), you might want to consider doing a little work to help improve the vibe!

5-MINUTE QUICK FIX

Make a list of everyone in your household and write down what you admire about them. Also, write down what you would like your family members to admire about you.

_____

_____

_____

_____

_____

_____

_____

_____

_____

_____

_____

_____

_____

_____

_____

_____

_____

5-MINUTE QUICK FIX

Make a list of everyone in your household and write down 2 ways you can show them respect today. These can be acts of kindness, compliments, or sharing your feelings.

_____

_____

_____

_____

_____

_____

_____

_____

_____

_____

_____

_____

_____

_____

_____

_____

_____

_____

_____

_____

_____

_____

10-MINUTE RESET

Carefully read each phrase three times out loud. Slowly repeat it as you inhale and exhale. Try looking in the mirror as you tell yourself these things!

"I am respected."

"I respect my parents and siblings."

"I am an important person in my family."

"My parents acknowledge me and respect me."

"I deeply care for my well-being and the well-being of others."

"I have a supportive family who loves me."

"I can respect my needs as well as the needs of others."

"I can be a kind person."

"Everyone in my family is important."

"My parents are happy and proud of me."

10-MINUTE RESET

Make two lists. On the first list, write out the feelings you have when you feel like your family isn't respecting you. On the second list, write about how you feel when your family shows you respect. Study the lists and circle the ones you like feeling the best.

_____

_____

_____

_____

_____

_____

_____

_____

_____

_____

_____

_____

_____

_____

_____

_____

_____

_____

_____

_____

15-MINUTE REGROUP

Write out three recent instances in which your parents have shown that they care about and love you. Make it a point to tell them "thank you" today.

_____

_____

_____

_____

_____

_____

_____

_____

_____

_____

_____

_____

_____

_____

_____

_____

_____

_____

15-MINUTE REGROUP

Think about the last time you felt disrespected at home or when you were disrespected. Reimagine the scene. What could have happened that would have changed the outcome for the better?

_____

_____

_____

_____

_____

_____

_____

_____

_____

_____

_____

_____

_____

_____

_____

_____

_____

_____

_____

_____

_____

_____

30-MINUTE DEEP DIVE

Sometimes, you may need to remind yourself to respect yourself. That means not telling yourself mean things in the mirror or allowing people to treat you in a way that makes you feel bad. It's important to practice self-love and respect in order to relieve anxious feelings about yourself.

Try this: Breathe deeply, inhale and exhale slowly.

a. Write down 10 things you love about yourself.

b. Write down 10 achievements you are proud of.

c. Write down 10 things you want to do this month to increase your happiness. (Include anything from hobbies that you enjoy doing to goals you wish to accomplish.)

d. Write down 10 things that make you happy.

_____

_____

_____

_____

_____

_____

_____

_____

_____

_____

_____

_____

30-MINUTE DEEP DIVE

Why are each of your family relationships important to you? What could you do better in each of these relationships, and what could they do better to increase your respect for one another?

_____

_____

_____

_____

_____

_____

_____

_____

_____

_____

_____

_____

_____

_____

_____

_____

_____

_____

_____

_____

_____

_____

"The best way to find out if you can trust somebody is to trust them."

— *Ernest Hemingway, American author*

TRUST

You trust those caring for you to look out for you, keep you fed, have a roof over your head, get you educated, and do what's best for you (the list goes on). And, those caring for you trust you to do well in school, make good choices, clean up after yourself, and love your siblings (this list also goes on). You might find that when someone in the family doesn't follow through with what they've said they are going to do, you lose faith and begin to doubt that you can trust them. This can cause needless anxiety.

Building trust between you and your family is very beneficial. If you say you will do a chore or get home at a certain time – do it! When you repeatedly do the opposite of what you say you will do, people will stop trusting you. The same goes for those caring for you. It's okay to hold them accountable as long as you hold yourself accountable, too.

Friend, don't forget: You really need to trust yourself. You are capable of making the right decisions, acing the test, winning the game, etc. Trust and confidence go hand in hand. And, when you trust your family and yourself, you might find that those anxious feelings go away.

5-MINUTE QUICK FIX

List 5 situations where you trust yourself the most. An example might be: "I will always apologize if something is my fault" or "I will never cheat on a test."

_____

_____

_____

_____

_____

_____

_____

_____

_____

_____

_____

_____

_____

_____

_____

_____

_____

_____

5-MINUTE QUICK FIX

What are some things your family members do that make it easy for you to trust them?

_____

_____

_____

_____

_____

_____

_____

_____

_____

_____

_____

_____

_____

_____

_____

_____

_____

_____

_____

_____

_____

10-MINUTE RESET

Repeat the following affirmations. Then, draw a doodle for each one!

"I trust myself, and I believe in myself."

"When I'm in an uncertain situation, I trust that I will make the right decision."

"I trust that my parents are making decisions in my best interest."

"I feel safe in my home."

"I know that I will be able to deal with stressful situations positively."

"My family can trust me to support them when they need it."

"I follow through with the promises I make."

"Others can trust me to be a source of strength in times of stress."

10-MINUTE RESET

Write about a time when you felt safe expressing yourself openly and honestly. Give a detailed account of that experience.

_____

_____

_____

_____

_____

_____

_____

_____

_____

_____

_____

_____

_____

_____

_____

_____

_____

_____

_____

_____

_____

_____

15-MINUTE REGROUP

List each family member and write down why you trust them. Write down the things you do to earn their trust.

_____

_____

_____

_____

_____

_____

_____

_____

_____

_____

_____

_____

_____

_____

_____

_____

_____

_____

_____

_____

15-MINUTE REGROUP

In the next month, what can your family expect from you? What can you expect from them?

_____

_____

_____

_____

_____

_____

_____

_____

_____

_____

_____

_____

_____

_____

_____

_____

_____

_____

_____

_____

_____

_____

30-MINUTE DEEP DIVE

Journal about a time when you broke a family member's or close friend's trust. What happened? What caused you to act the way you did? How did you fix the situation?

_____

_____

_____

_____

_____

_____

_____

_____

_____

_____

_____

_____

_____

_____

_____

_____

_____

_____

_____

30-MINUTE DEEP DIVE

Journal about a time when a family member or close friend broke your trust. What happened? What do you think caused them to act the way they did? How did they fix the situation?

_____

_____

_____

_____

_____

_____

_____

_____

_____

_____

_____

_____

_____

_____

_____

_____

_____

_____

_____

_____

_____

_____

"I learned a long time ago the wisest thing I can do is be on my own side, be an advocate for myself and others like me."

— *Maya Angelou, American memoirist*

ADVOCATE

Speak now, and don't forever hold your peace. Speaking up for yourself is one way to support yourself. When you need your family to be there for you, when you need time alone, when you need to be listened to, or when you need help because things have gotten really stressful for you – advocating for yourself is important. It simply means that you are voicing your needs and feelings. When you don't, THINGS...GET...CRAZY. Feelings and problems can fester like big ol' pimples! (Just go away, already...)

In the section before, we talked about trust. Voice your needs to someone in your family that you trust without fear of getting in trouble for being honest. Find that voice, and don't be afraid to communicate what you need. You'll feel calmer and in control when you show up for yourself, just as you would for a friend in need. *Friend, remember that every friend to someone needs someone to be a friend to them.*

5-MINUTE QUICK FIX

Carefully read each phrase three times out loud. Slowly repeat it as you inhale and exhale. Try looking in the mirror as you tell yourself these things!

"I know that I am allowed to speak up when I feel like I need something."

"If I have a question, I know that my parents/teacher/friends/etc. will listen."

"I know that my needs are important to them."

"If I ask my parents for something, they will listen and comfort me."

"It's okay to feel comfortable speaking up. I believe in myself."

"I am learning to say no when I need to and taking care of myself more so that I have the energy to take care of others."

5-MINUTE QUICK FIX

Write down ten things that you need to feel safe, calm, and in control.
Who can you ask to provide those things for you?

_____

_____

_____

_____

_____

_____

_____

_____

_____

_____

_____

_____

_____

_____

_____

_____

_____

_____

_____

_____

10-MINUTE RESET

Think about something at home that you are struggling with currently; maybe it is something that is causing you stress or making you feel anxious. How can you advocate for yourself to make the situation better? Who can you talk to? How can your family members help you through this situation?

_____

_____

_____

_____

_____

_____

_____

_____

_____

_____

_____

_____

_____

_____

_____

_____

_____

_____

_____

10-MINUTE RESET

It is okay to feel some stress or anxiety (that means you care) — but it can become a problem if that stress causes you to shut down, become sad, make unhealthy choices, or treat people unkindly. List 5 things you need help with this week and who you can ask to support you.

_____

_____

_____

_____

_____

_____

_____

_____

_____

_____

_____

_____

_____

_____

_____

_____

_____

_____

_____

_____

15-MINUTE REGROUP

Think about your favorite movie or novel where the main character has a struggle. How did you learn they were struggling? How did they solve the problem? List three things you learned from their situation.

_____

_____

_____

_____

_____

_____

_____

_____

_____

_____

_____

_____

_____

_____

_____

_____

_____

_____

15-MINUTE REGROUP

Write down at least five things you'd like to have comfort in while talking to a family member or close friend. Pick one thing on the list that is not something you'd typically ask for help with. Take action on it by asking them for it within the next few days. If this goes well, add another thing from your list so that you can continue to work towards taking care of yourself.

_____

_____

_____

_____

_____

_____

_____

_____

_____

_____

_____

_____

_____

_____

_____

_____

_____

_____

_____

_____

30-MINUTE DEEP DIVE

Pick at least three things you would like to accomplish in the next 30 days. What will you need from your family members to make that happen? Make a list of steps for each goal that includes what you need to do each week to accomplish it.

_____

_____

_____

_____

_____

_____

_____

_____

_____

_____

_____

_____

_____

_____

_____

_____

_____

_____

_____

_____

30-MINUTE DEEP DIVE

Is there a member of your family that needs your support? How can you advocate for them? Would they benefit from you speaking up regarding their needs? How does your voice at home help your family members when they need it?

_____

_____

_____

_____

_____

_____

_____

_____

_____

_____

_____

_____

_____

_____

_____

_____

_____

_____

_____

_____

_____

_____

"Carry out a random act of kindness, with no expectation of reward, safe in the knowledge that one day someone might do the same for you."

— *Diana, Princess of Wales*

EMPATHIZE

It can be hard to understand other people's needs because you may not have the same experiences as them or you don't find interest or value in the same things. But that doesn't mean you can't try. Empathy means imagining what your loved one is going through. It can help them (and you!) feel calm and supported.

When you imagine being someone else, you might find it easier to understand their feelings and, in return, adjust how you interact with them. Taking time to patiently listen (without scrolling through your social media or staring at the big screen) and ask questions about what they might need can help them feel more calm and able to deal with anxious thoughts. Sometimes showing empathy towards others can help them become more empathetic themselves.

5-MINUTE QUICK FIX

Make a list of 5 things a family member has gone through that you haven't experienced. These are moments where you can seek to better understand them.

_____

_____

_____

_____

_____

_____

_____

_____

_____

_____

_____

_____

_____

_____

_____

_____

_____

_____

_____

_____

5-MINUTE QUICK FIX

Make a list of 5 things you have experienced that no one in your family has dealt with. These are moments where you can seek for them to better understand you.

_____

_____

_____

_____

_____

_____

_____

_____

_____

_____

_____

_____

_____

_____

_____

_____

_____

_____

_____

_____

_____

_____

10-MINUTE RESET

Repeat the following affirmations. Then, draw a doodle for each one!

"I am becoming a more empathetic person."

"I enjoy being around my family members."

"I am always concerned about what my family members are going through."

"I can listen with compassion, acceptance, and curiosity in order to help people feel better."

10-MINUTE RESET

List 5 things you wish you had from your family members. Then, take each statement and write an empathic response to why they might not be meeting your expectations. Lastly, write an action that can demonstrate your understanding of their situation.

Example:

Wish: I wish my sister had more time to hang out with me.

Empathetic Response: I understand that my sister is taking two extra classes and has to dedicate more time to studying, so she doesn't have as much time to hang with me.

Action: Next time my sister has a study session, I'm going to bring her a snack and ask her if I can help in any way.

_____

_____

_____

_____

_____

_____

_____

_____

_____

_____

_____

_____

_____

_____

15-MINUTE REGROUP

In a stressful situation, it can be easy to react with anger, which can cause more conflict. Instead of reacting to someone's anger or other negative emotions, you can practice showing them empathy by saying things like "I'm sorry," "It's okay," or "How can I help?" Think about a recent time when you could have been more empathetic towards your family or loved ones, and journal about it below.

_____

_____

_____

_____

_____

_____

_____

_____

_____

_____

_____

_____

_____

_____

_____

_____

15-MINUTE REGROUP

Think about what your loved ones are going through or might be going through in the future and plan how you can help them get through the situation.

_____

_____

_____

_____

_____

_____

_____

_____

_____

_____

_____

_____

_____

_____

_____

_____

_____

_____

_____

_____

_____

_____

_____

30-MINUTE DEEP DIVE

Make a list of 10 things that cause you anger or anxiety within yourself. Channel your thoughts from anger and anxiety into empathy and sympathy and write new feelings to explore so that you can understand, listen and offer help to yourself, just as you would a family member or best friend.

_____

_____

_____

_____

_____

_____

_____

_____

_____

_____

_____

_____

_____

_____

_____

_____

_____

_____

_____

_____

_____

_____

30-MINUTE DEEP DIVE

Choose a family member or loved one that you know is dealing with a stressful situation. What assumptions will you abandon that allow you to be more empathetic? Example: assuming that they are fine because they seem strong or don't need help because they haven't asked...

_____

_____

_____

_____

_____

_____

_____

_____

_____

_____

_____

_____

_____

_____

_____

_____

_____

_____

_____

_____

_____

_____

"The quality of your life will be determined by the quality of your contribution. When you work to improve the lives of others, your life improves automatically."

— *Kurek Ashley, Author + Inspirational Speaker*

CONTRIBUTE

No one gets anywhere by themselves. Humans are communal creatures. Even though you might be feeling like a superhero and that you can do it all alone, it's not sustainable. You know the drill: "It takes a village," "There's no I in team," and yadda yadda.

We gotta help each other out and try to pitch in for the people we love. This is very important in the household. It feels comfortable to have a clean house. It feels nice when everyone has a role. It lessens stress when things get taken care of without sighs or grunts.

Chores, sh-mores. But you have a lot to give, Friend. Get a routine, offer your strengths, and you'll see that you, your parents, and your family members will motivate each other to keep a happy and healthy home. It's like your first real job in life: Do your part.

5-MINUTE QUICK FIX

Think about your household and list what you can do to help. Now, categorize those chores and tasks you can finish in five minutes, 10 minutes, and 30 minutes.

_____

_____

_____

_____

_____

_____

_____

_____

_____

_____

_____

_____

_____

_____

_____

_____

5-MINUTE QUICK FIX

Carefully read each phrase three times out loud. Slowly repeat it as you inhale and exhale. Try looking in the mirror as you tell yourself these things!

"I know that I can pitch in whenever I'm needed."

"I know that it's important for me to pitch in when I have time.

"I understand that I can help out by doing any kind of chores that are needed."

"I am contributing in my own way, and it feels good."

"I am realizing I have abilities I didn't realize before."

"I am fixing problems within my household in my own way and becoming more productive daily.

"I am contributing in the ways that I can."

10-MINUTE RESET

List ways you can be a productive part of your family or community with your specific talents and skills. What are you good at? Organizing? Speed cleaning? Planning grocery lists? Cooking? Volunteering?

_____

_____

_____

_____

_____

_____

_____

_____

_____

_____

_____

_____

_____

_____

_____

_____

_____

10-MINUTE RESET

What have you done this week to contribute to the household? How did it help you and your family? What went well? What didn't go well? What were your successes from this week? And, what do you want to work on more?

_____

_____

_____

_____

_____

_____

_____

_____

_____

_____

_____

_____

_____

_____

_____

_____

_____

_____

_____

_____

_____

_____

_____

15-MINUTE REGROUP

Write down little tasks or ideas you would like to see implemented in your household that could make it run happier or smoother.

_____

_____

_____

_____

_____

_____

_____

_____

_____

_____

_____

_____

_____

_____

_____

_____

_____

_____

_____

_____

15-MINUTE REGROUP

Outside of household chores, what other ways can you contribute to your family to help make things easier? Commit to planning and completing a few items on your list.

_____

_____

_____

_____

_____

_____

_____

_____

_____

_____

_____

_____

_____

_____

_____

_____

_____

_____

_____

_____

_____

_____

30-MINUTE DEEP DIVE

How would you like to contribute to your community in the future? What kinds of careers are you considering, and what kinds of contributions would you be making in order to be a successful participant?

_____

_____

_____

_____

_____

_____

_____

_____

_____

_____

_____

_____

_____

_____

_____

_____

_____

_____

_____

_____

_____

_____

30-MINUTE DEEP DIVE

Write about a time when everyone in your family contributed. How did that make you feel? How did it relieve the stress and anxiety?

_____

_____

_____

_____

_____

_____

_____

_____

_____

_____

_____

_____

_____

_____

_____

_____

_____

_____

_____

_____

_____

_____

CHAPTER 2: I AM SMART

Friend, are you stressed at school? The pressure to perform well in school can cause a great deal of stress and anxiety. At this point in your life, you've heard how important it is to get a good education — whether that's at a 4-year college, a community college, or a trade school. Your parents might often reward you for good grades or take away privileges (Not my phone, puh-leeeeezeeee!) if your report card is sprinkled with a few different letters from the alphabet. Some anxiety is beneficial — it's the reason you study for tests and care about what your teachers think. But, too much stress around your education can backfire — you might freeze up on tests or presentations, adopt unhealthy ways to cope, or beat yourself up for making mistakes that, in the big scheme of things, aren't as detrimental to your success as you might think.

In this chapter, we'll practice these five values, which can lead to a more level-headed and prepared educational experience. (It is possible!)

Dream: Knowing why you are working toward an educational goal is key to balancing your expectations with your reality.

Plan: Thinking about the best way to approach your studies will help you feel calmer and more prepared when you're faced with challenging tasks.

Balance: Understanding your limits and capacity can help prevent you from taking on more than you can handle — which can cause unnecessary stress and anxiety.

Believe: Having confidence in yourself to do your best can help you weather the many ups and downs of the school year.

Achieve: Allowing yourself to celebrate your success can build your self-esteem and encourage you to attempt challenges that you normally would avoid out of fear of defeat.

Exploring these values can help you navigate your educational endeavors with confidence, humility, and grace to avoid the cycle of anxiety that can happen with what seems like a never-ending school year. And remember, Friend, while your grades are important, they are NOT more important than your mental health and well-being.

"Everyone's dream can come true if you just stick to it and work hard."

— *Serena Williams, American tennis player*

DREAM

It is important for you to set reasonable educational goals, especially since, as teenagers, our goals are not always realistic. You hear it all the time: You can do ANYTHING you put your mind to — which can be true! But you can't do EVERYTHING you put your mind to — it's just not possible.

So, let's get to work discovering your dreams, your strengths, and your weaknesses so that they can help you determine where to put your energy. What do you really want to do?

I AM SMART

5-MINUTE QUICK FIX

Make a list of your 5 biggest strengths as a student and 5 things you would like to improve during this school year.

_____

_____

_____

_____

_____

_____

_____

_____

_____

_____

_____

_____

_____

_____

_____

_____

_____

_____

_____

_____

5-MINUTE QUICK FIX

Turn on your favorite song, think about some of your biggest dreams, and use this page to doodle.

I AM SMART

10-MINUTE RESET

Think about five educational goals you would like to accomplish within a year and why you want to achieve them. How will your strengths help you achieve these goals?

_____

_____

_____

_____

_____

_____

_____

_____

_____

_____

_____

_____

_____

_____

_____

_____

_____

_____

_____

_____

_____

_____

10-MINUTE RESET

Make a list of topics/studies that you are NOT interested in. It sounds crazy, but it's important to know what might not be worth investing your time in.

_____

_____

_____

_____

_____

_____

_____

_____

_____

_____

_____

_____

_____

_____

_____

_____

_____

_____

_____

_____

I AM SMART

15-MINUTE REGROUP

Open up a browser and do a career search. Look through all the different types of careers, businesses, organizations, and passions. List out the ones that interest you. Circle the ones that complement your strengths.

_____

_____

_____

_____

_____

_____

_____

_____

_____

_____

_____

_____

_____

_____

_____

_____

_____

_____

_____

15-MINUTE REGROUP

Who are some of your role models? Why? Are they living your dreams? How do you think they got where they are today?

_____

_____

_____

_____

_____

_____

_____

_____

_____

_____

_____

_____

_____

_____

_____

_____

_____

_____

_____

_____

_____

I AM SMART

30-MINUTE DEEP DIVE

Find two people that you admire and talk to them about their educational journeys and how they got to where they are today. Do their journeys surprise you? What are some exciting things you learned?

_____

_____

_____

_____

_____

_____

_____

_____

_____

_____

_____

_____

_____

_____

_____

_____

_____

_____

30-MINUTE DEEP DIVE

Make a detailed list of goals. Categorize them by short-term, mid-term, and long-term. Choose urgent, realistic, and achievable ones so you'll have the confidence and energy to follow through.

_____

_____

_____

_____

_____

_____

_____

_____

_____

_____

_____

_____

_____

_____

_____

_____

_____

_____

_____

_____

_____

_____

_____

I AM SMART

"Always have a plan, and believe in it. Nothing happens by accident."

— *Chuck Knox, former NFL head coach*

PLAN

Ready...Set...Start! The easiest way to get something done is to start. One foot in front of the other. It can save you a few headaches here and there if you take time to plan — for a test, for a class project, for failure, for breakfast. If you can name it, you can plan for it. Many times, anxiety can result from not thinking about how something will turn out or not having a plan for the various outcomes.

One way to jump into a planning mindset is to think of things in terms of a timeline. What is the goal, and what steps must be taken to complete it? Slice big tasks into smaller chunks. Just by making a list of steps, you can remove a layer of anxiety. Imagine ordering a giant pizza. You don't just eat the whole pizza at once. You eat it slice by slice until the entire pizza is gone. Conquer your smaller goals step by step until the giant goal is accomplished.

Once you have actionable steps for your goals, projects, or tasks, it's time to identify any areas you might need support. Tell your family you've got a big project on your plate. Ask your teacher for additional tutoring sessions. Take a break from extracurriculars if you know you will need the extra time. All of these things can't be done after the fact — but if you lay out your needs and do a little planning, you can eliminate many obstacles to your success.

I AM SMART

5-MINUTE QUICK FIX

Make a list of your current priorities. Choose the scariest on your list and quickly write down all the steps that have to happen for you to complete it.

_____

_____

_____

_____

_____

_____

_____

_____

_____

_____

_____

_____

_____

_____

_____

_____

_____

_____

5-MINUTE QUICK FIX

What are some things that you are really good at planning?

_____

_____

_____

_____

_____

_____

_____

_____

_____

_____

_____

_____

_____

_____

_____

_____

_____

_____

_____

_____

_____

I AM SMART

10-MINUTE RESET

Think of a time when you were really nervous at school. (Or maybe you are having that moment right now!) What is/was causing this anxiety? List the reasons why you aren't feeling calm. Could you have done something to help your nerves before this moment?

_____

_____

_____

_____

_____

_____

_____

_____

_____

_____

_____

_____

_____

_____

_____

_____

_____

_____

_____

_____

10-MINUTE RESET

Carefully read each phrase three times out loud. Slowly repeat it as you inhale and exhale. Try looking in the mirror as you tell yourself these things!

"A plan in place will make me feel calm."

"Successful people make plans."

"I want to be able to focus on the present so that I can make the most of my day."

"I will manage my time better and not get carried away with too many things at once."

"I will be mindful of my emotions and feelings so that I don't get myself into situations I cannot handle."

"If I make a plan, I can handle anything."

"Planning can help me achieve my goals."

"Before I start any project, I will list the steps and make a plan."

15-MINUTE REGROUP

Set a timer. Find an activity that is very relaxing for you. Put your favorite music on, and get to work. Think about the steps you are taking as you complete this activity.

_____

_____

_____

_____

_____

_____

_____

_____

_____

_____

_____

_____

_____

_____

_____

_____

_____

_____

_____

15-MINUTE REGROUP

List 5 situations where you could have planned better. Maybe you made a plan, but you think you can improve on it next time. Or, you didn't make a plan, but now you know that you will make one next time. What was the result? Did you feel prepared in advance? How will you change or improve your plan next time?

_____

_____

_____

_____

_____

_____

_____

_____

_____

_____

_____

_____

_____

_____

_____

_____

_____

_____

_____

_____

I AM SMART

30-MINUTE DEEP DIVE

Find a quiet place and journal about the following:

1. What are my goals and how can I achieve these goals?

2. What is important to me at the moment? (family, friends, school, health, etc.)

3. Why do I even bother? (Why is it important for me to change?)

_____

_____

_____

_____

_____

_____

_____

_____

_____

_____

_____

_____

_____

_____

_____

_____

_____

_____

_____

30-MINUTE DEEP DIVE

Time to plan! Make a list of all the things you need to complete this week. Then, for each item, write out the steps you have to take for each and schedule work time on your calendar to knock them out!

_____

_____

_____

_____

_____

_____

_____

_____

_____

_____

_____

_____

_____

_____

_____

_____

_____

_____

_____

_____

I AM SMART

"It's important to have balance in your life between work and play."

— *Bobby Flay, American chef*

BALANCE

When you're being pulled in too many directions, you may feel like you aren't doing anything well. That is the feeling of being off-balance — you're saying yes to too many things, and it is causing A LOT of stress. It may seem impossible to think you can be a healthy eater, get proper sleep and exercise, make the grades you want, and have a bumpin' social life. But you can do all of these things with a balanced approach!

The key is to continually assess your commitments. Can you reasonably achieve the things you've committed to? What are the most important things for you to do this week? What can you drop so you can get a better night's sleep or hang out with your family? You may not always be able to achieve a perfect balance. Still, by limiting stress-inducing commitments, your week will feel more manageable.

Think of your time and energy like a gas tank — there's only so much fuel, and you can't drive with the same tank forever. Eating a balanced diet, getting proper sleep, and exercising a few times a week is the equivalent of stopping at the gas station to recharge and take a break (go ahead, get that Snickers bar, too).

I AM SMART

5-MINUTE QUICK FIX

Find your center — breathe!

i) Close your eyes.

ii) Try to empty your mind.

iii) Breath into the lower abdomen area, loosening the belly and allowing relaxation and decompression to come through you.

iv) Relieve any tension in the body by forcing yourself to breathe deeply into a more relaxed area.

v) Continue until you feel relaxed and alert at the same time.

5-MINUTE QUICK FIX

Write about something that you can change, adjust, eliminate or add to your life to gain balance.

_____

_____

_____

_____

_____

_____

_____

_____

_____

_____

_____

_____

_____

_____

_____

_____

_____

_____

_____

_____

I AM SMART

10-MINUTE RESET

What does having a balanced life look like? Write down how your life would be if it had more balance.

_____

_____

_____

_____

_____

_____

_____

_____

_____

_____

_____

_____

_____

_____

_____

_____

_____

_____

_____

_____

_____

10-MINUTE RESET

Repeat the following affirmations. Then, draw a doodle for each one!

"I strive for balance so that I can keep my commitments."

"I am a balanced person who knows my limits."

"I feel centered."

"The world needs me to stay balanced, so I can live up to my potential."

"I know that if I feel unbalanced, I know what to do to get back on track."

"My teachers are supportive of me, and they want me to have balance. I don't have to participate in every activity."

"Having a balanced schedule keeps me calm."

15-MINUTE REGROUP

Pretend your friend comes to you for help because they feel their life is unbalanced. What advice would you give your friend?

_____

_____

_____

_____

_____

_____

_____

_____

_____

_____

_____

_____

_____

_____

_____

_____

15-MINUTE REGROUP

Write down at least five things you'd like to have that would contribute to a more balanced schedule at school. What do you need to do to get those things?

_____

_____

_____

_____

_____

_____

_____

_____

_____

_____

_____

_____

_____

_____

_____

_____

_____

_____

_____

_____

_____

_____

I AM SMART

30-MINUTE DEEP DIVE

Think about something at school you are struggling with currently (something that is causing you stress or making you feel anxious). How can you create more balance for yourself to make the situation better? Who can you talk to? How can mentors at school help you through this situation?

_____

_____

_____

_____

_____

_____

_____

_____

_____

_____

_____

_____

_____

_____

_____

_____

_____

_____

_____

30-MINUTE DEEP DIVE

List all of your commitments for next week and how much time each one will take. Then, look at your calendar and determine how much time you have to dedicate to these commitments outside of your usual set schedule. Include the hours you need to sleep, eat, and exercise. How do the hours you need compare to the hours you have?

_____

_____

_____

_____

_____

_____

_____

_____

_____

_____

_____

_____

_____

_____

_____

_____

_____

_____

_____

_____

"Always remember you are braver than you believe, stronger than you seem, and smarter than you think."

— *Christopher Robin, Adventures with Winnie-the-Pooh*

BELIEVE

You can do it! Do you believe you can do it? Learning to believe in yourself is the most significant skill you'll need to get through those long, tough school days. Having faith in yourself will help you bounce back from failure and get back into the game. Don't let one failure stop your entire plan; take a few minutes to think about what might have gone wrong and then move on.

Trusting yourself takes guts, especially when you need to defend yourself from unkind remarks, make difficult decisions with friends, or believe that what you're doing is right. But, you know yourself best. You have the guts! Listen to your heart, revisit your values often, have a pep rally with yourself daily, and NEVER...GIVE...UP.

I AM SMART

5-MINUTE QUICK FIX

Write about a situation where you failed or succeeded, and think about why this happened.

_____

_____

_____

_____

_____

_____

_____

_____

_____

_____

_____

_____

_____

_____

_____

_____

_____

_____

_____

_____

5-MINUTE QUICK FIX

Write down or search for your favorite quotes to remind yourself that you can do great things.

_____

_____

_____

_____

_____

_____

_____

_____

_____

_____

_____

_____

_____

_____

_____

_____

_____

_____

_____

_____

_____

_____

I AM SMART

10-MINUTE RESET

Make a list of 10 things you believe about yourself that can keep you motivated when you face challenges at school.

_____

_____

_____

_____

_____

_____

_____

_____

_____

_____

_____

_____

_____

_____

_____

_____

_____

_____

_____

_____

_____

_____

10-MINUTE RESET

Carefully read each phrase three times out loud. Slowly repeat it as you inhale and exhale. Try looking in the mirror as you tell yourself these things!

"I believe in myself, even though I have made mistakes, and I can learn from them."

"I am a strong person who has the power to turn my situation around."

"I have a voice, and I am capable of being heard."

"The world needs me, and I am capable of making a difference in it."

"I accept my flaws and strengths; that makes me who I am."

"My parents are supportive of me, and they love me. We are on the same team. Together we can make a difference."

"My friends and family love me and want the best for me."

I AM SMART

15-MINUTE REGROUP

Think about a mentor/someone who believes in you and helps you believe that you can accomplish anything. Write them a letter here to tell them how much they helped you. You can send it to them if you'd like!

_____

_____

_____

_____

_____

_____

_____

_____

_____

_____

_____

_____

_____

_____

_____

_____

_____

_____

_____

_____

15-MINUTE REGROUP

Write about a situation in school where you wish you had trusted yourself more. When did you start to doubt yourself? Why do you think you didn't trust or believe in yourself? How will it look next time when you face this same situation with belief and trust in yourself?

_____

_____

_____

_____

_____

_____

_____

_____

_____

_____

_____

_____

_____

_____

_____

_____

_____

_____

_____

I AM SMART

30-MINUTE DEEP DIVE

Set a timer for half an hour. Answer as many of the prompts below:

Describe your ideal confident self. What are you wearing, how do you feel, what are you doing?

Name three qualities that make students seem confident. What would you need to do to feel that way?

Talk about a time at school when you felt really confident. What happened? Describe your actions and reactions.

Describe situations in class or at school that make you feel less confident. Who was involved? What class or activity were you in? Did you feel prepared?

_____

_____

_____

_____

_____

_____

_____

_____

_____

_____

_____

_____

_____

30-MINUTE DEEP DIVE

Draw 12 circles. In six of the circles, write down nouns/adjectives that describe you when you feel confident. In the other six, write down nouns/adjectives that describe you when you feel doubtful.

For the six doubtful circles, write a solution for how to overcome that feeling. How can you think differently?

I AM SMART

"I realized that if I was going to achieve anything in life I had to be aggressive. I had to get out there and go for it."

— *Michael Jordan, American former basketball player*

ACHIEVE

There is no doubt that one of your goals is to be successful in the world, but success can look very different for each person. It can be helpful to first define what success looks like to you. Does it mean getting into the best college, making lots of money, becoming an influencer on social media, volunteering each summer break, starting a business, or taking trips? You may think that being the best is the only achievement, but there are so many ways to achieve — from making it all the way through, learning how to bounce back, and working through challenges... it's not always about being the best. You are valuable either way.

Friend, let's explore what you're doing all this work for! And I'm sure there are supportive people in your life that want to see you achieve your dreams.

I AM SMART

5-MINUTE QUICK FIX

Visualize a point in your future where you have achieved something you've worked for. Describe the details about how you did it, how you feel, how your life has changed, etc.

_____

_____

_____

_____

_____

_____

_____

_____

_____

_____

_____

_____

_____

_____

_____

_____

_____

_____

_____

_____

5-MINUTE QUICK FIX

Make a list of all of the things you achieved in the last school year and assign a number to them according to the effort you put in. 1 (Low Effort) 2 (Medium Effort) 3 (High Effort). How many high-effort goals did you attempt last year?

_____
_____
_____
_____
_____
_____
_____
_____
_____
_____
_____
_____
_____
_____
_____
_____
_____
_____

I AM SMART

10-MINUTE RESET

Turn on your favorite song! Use this page to doodle while you envision achieving something you've been working on at school.

10-MINUTE RESET

Talk about the most challenging achievement you accomplished last school year. What are you most proud of?

_____

_____

_____

_____

_____

_____

_____

_____

_____

_____

_____

_____

_____

_____

_____

_____

_____

_____

I AM SMART

15-MINUTE REGROUP

Repeat the following affirmations. Then, draw a doodle for each one!

"I can achieve goals if I put in the work."

"Even if I don't get the results I want, I'll still be happy I tried."

"I am an achiever. I work hard. I'll keep trying."

"I am talented and can achieve good things."

"I deserve good things happening to me."

"My teachers want good things for me and will help me achieve my goals."

15-MINUTE REGROUP

List all of your strengths that help you get close to your goal. Have these strengths always been there, or did you learn them through other experiences?

_____

_____

_____

_____

_____

_____

_____

_____

_____

_____

_____

_____

_____

_____

_____

_____

_____

_____

_____

_____

I AM SMART

30-MINUTE DEEP DIVE

Imagine if you achieved something in everything you did at school. List five times at school that you didn't reach your goal. Now, think about what you did achieve, even if it wasn't what you were aiming for. For example, did you learn a new skill? Did you reach a new level of understanding? Did you find ways to improve upon your current process? Find a way to win in all five examples.

_____

_____

_____

_____

_____

_____

_____

_____

_____

_____

_____

_____

_____

_____

_____

_____

_____

_____

30-MINUTE DEEP DIVE

Make a playlist of 10 songs that celebrate achievements. Write the titles below. And make sure to blast this playlist multiple times per week to keep you on a winning path!

_____

_____

_____

_____

_____

_____

_____

_____

_____

_____

_____

_____

_____

_____

_____

_____

_____

_____

I AM SMART

CHAPTER 3: I AM WORTHY

You likely have A LOT of feelings surrounding your friends and social circle. There are pressures from social media, movies/television, friends, and people you're attracted to. These cultural pressures can be challenging to handle because you're discovering who you are, all while it seems like every minute, people are trying to shape you into what's popular. There is no worse feeling than a sense of not belonging, but you don't have to do things that feel outside of your character to impress people.

Friend, it is cooler to be true to who you are. Find people who don't require you to change who you are to gain their approval. Find friends who like you for your interests and personality instead of something you've imitated from the social media accounts you follow and the characters on television that "seem" cool.

In this chapter, we'll practice these five values, which can lead to a more confident and healthy social circle.

Support: Find your people. Your teenage years will move fast, but you need good solid friends to help you create lasting memories that you can look back on and be proud of.

Celebrate: When good things happen to the people you love, be happy for them. You'll find that when you lift people up, they will return the favor.

Include: You know what it feels like to be left out. When you create situations where people feel included instead of excluded, you'll feel gratitude for all the people that make up our world.

Defend: Learning how to defend yourself, and your friends (or someone experiencing wrongdoing) is a lifelong skill. Shedding light on injustice can create feelings of purpose and self-worth.

Evaluate: Try to avoid jumping into situations blindly. Always assess pros and cons, risks and rewards, and whether or not what you're feeling in the moment will matter in a day, a month, or 5 years.

Exploring these values can help you build a supportive group of friends who allow you to be you, support you when you need it, and make you feel good about yourself and your decisions.

"We can improve our relationships with others by leaps and bounds if we become encouragers instead of critics."

– *Joyce Meyer, American author*

SUPPORT

Friend, I bet you are happier when you are with your friends and family. Studies show that having healthy relationships can lead to a happier existence. Feeling supported by friends and family gives you the strength to cope when life feels anxious or stressful. And, when your friend circle is healthy, you'll likely feel calmer and more confident in your day-to-day activities.

People with negative or destructive behaviors, no matter how popular they are, might cause you unnecessary stress on top of everything else you have going on. You know what we're talking about: people who gossip, people who are selfish with your time, people who take more than they give, people who act before thinking, and people who get angry easily. None of these behaviors contribute to a healthy friendship if they are repeated without remorse. And you won't make a good friend if you act this way, either.

I AM WORTHY

5-MINUTE QUICK FIX

Write three ways that you can be supportive of your friends. Then, write three ways that your friends can be supportive of you.

_____

_____

_____

_____

_____

_____

_____

_____

_____

_____

_____

_____

_____

_____

_____

_____

_____

5-MINUTE QUICK FIX

Make a list of all the people in your community who support you fully. This could be at school, church, clubs — anyone you know who has your back when things get tough.

_____

_____

_____

_____

_____

_____

_____

_____

_____

_____

_____

_____

_____

_____

_____

_____

_____

_____

_____

I AM WORTHY

10-MINUTE RESET

Think about a time when you were not feeling good, and one of your friends gave you support. How did they help make you feel better?

_____

_____

_____

_____

_____

_____

_____

_____

_____

_____

_____

_____

_____

_____

_____

_____

_____

_____

_____

10-MINUTE RESET

Carefully read each phrase three times out loud. Slowly repeat it as you inhale and exhale. Try looking in the mirror as you tell yourself these things!

"I am loved and supported."

"I love and accept myself."

"I am a good friend."

"I have a great time with my friends."

"I deserve friends who are genuine and want the best for me."

"I am a supportive friend."

"My friends treat me with respect."

I AM WORTHY

15-MINUTE REGROUP

Write about a time when a friend was not supportive of you. How did you feel, and why do you think this happened?

_____

_____

_____

_____

_____

_____

_____

_____

_____

_____

_____

_____

_____

_____

_____

_____

_____

_____

_____

_____

15-MINUTE REGROUP

What are some areas of your social life where you might need more support? Are you struggling with making friends, gossiping, or not saying the right things? What steps can you take to get more support in those areas?

_____

_____

_____

_____

_____

_____

_____

_____

_____

_____

_____

_____

_____

_____

_____

_____

_____

_____

I AM WORTHY

30-MINUTE DEEP-DIVE

What are the qualities that make up a good friend? Once you have a list of at least five, journal about how you could improve yourself in each quality you wrote.

_____

_____

_____

_____

_____

_____

_____

_____

_____

_____

_____

_____

_____

_____

_____

_____

_____

_____

_____

_____

_____

_____

30-MINUTE DEEP-DIVE

How far is too far when it comes to supporting your friend? Write about a time when you should have ended a friendship sooner than you did. What happened? How did it make you feel?

_____

_____

_____

_____

_____

_____

_____

_____

_____

_____

_____

_____

_____

_____

_____

_____

_____

_____

_____

_____

_____

_____

I AM WORTHY

"I embrace the imperfections and celebrate them."

– *Kesha, American singer-songwriter*

CELEBRATE

WOOHOO... LET'S PARTY!!!!! It's SO important to remember to congratulate and celebrate when you and your friends do big and small things. You might feel shy calling attention to that fantastic presentation you and your group worked on for weeks or to the fifth week in a row that you kept your room clean. But it is beneficial to acknowledge the times in life when you came through for yourself. And this works for your social circle, too. Celebrating your friends' successes and differences can keep everyone's self-esteem and confidence healthy.

Even celebrating small victories can help you realize that even though you might not have everything figured out just yet, you keep knocking it out of the park on the daily stuff that matters.

I AM WORTHY

5-MINUTE QUICK FIX

Write down 5 relationships that you have that are worth celebrating.
Why are they so special?

_____

_____

_____

_____

_____

_____

_____

_____

_____

_____

_____

_____

_____

_____

_____

_____

_____

_____

_____

_____

5-MINUTE QUICK FIX

Think about the big and small things you accomplished last month. How can you reward/celebrate yourself for those things?

_____

_____

_____

_____

_____

_____

_____

_____

_____

_____

_____

_____

_____

_____

_____

_____

_____

_____

_____

_____

I AM WORTHY

10-MINUTE RESET

Think about all the things you do in your life that you don't get rewarded for. Does that make you not want to do them? Why bother?

_____

_____

_____

_____

_____

_____

_____

_____

_____

_____

_____

_____

_____

_____

_____

_____

_____

_____

_____

_____

10-MINUTE RESET

Think of one friend who has done something extraordinary in the last month. Brainstorm below how you can celebrate them.

_____

_____

_____

_____

_____

_____

_____

_____

_____

_____

_____

_____

_____

_____

_____

_____

_____

_____

_____

_____

I AM WORTHY

15-MINUTE REGROUP

Repeat the following affirmations. Then, draw a doodle for each one!

"I deserve to be acknowledged."

"I celebrate myself and my actions every day."

"When someone does something amazing, I'll tell them."

"I enjoy celebrating other people."

"It's important to acknowledge big and small wins."

"I am calmer when I'm mindful about good things that happen."

"Small wins are worth celebrating."

"I'm happy when I acknowledge the good things I do."

15-MINUTE REGROUP

Journal about the last time you had a challenging situation. What were the positives in this situation? How can you focus on the good that came from facing this challenge?

_____

_____

_____

_____

_____

_____

_____

_____

_____

_____

_____

_____

_____

_____

_____

_____

_____

_____

_____

_____

I AM WORTHY

30-MINUTE DEEP-DIVE

Make a list of people who make you feel good about yourself and inspire you. Write how each person helps lift up your spirits.

_____

_____

_____

_____

_____

_____

_____

_____

_____

_____

_____

_____

_____

_____

_____

_____

_____

_____

_____

_____

_____

_____

_____

30-MINUTE DEEP-DIVE

Describe your perfect day outside of all of your current responsibilities. When you wake up, what's the first thing you do? Where do you go? Who do you spend it with? Walk through all of your waking hours and plan what it would look like if you could choose every moment.

_____

_____

_____

_____

_____

_____

_____

_____

_____

_____

_____

_____

_____

_____

_____

_____

_____

_____

_____

I AM WORTHY

"Giving connects two people, the giver and the receiver, and this connection gives birth to a new sense of belonging."

— *Deepak Chopra, Indian-American author*

INCLUDE

Friend, first things first, remember this...EVERYONE MATTERS, INCLUDING YOU! Everyone wants to feel a sense of belonging. However, sometimes we might feel like we are left out or that our opinions don't matter. (Newsflash: They DO.) Unfortunately, we can also make other people feel like their opinions don't matter. Being exclusive in your relationships can make people who don't know you feel like they can't approach you. And, when you have to work with different personalities, it can be hard to relate to them all. But luckily, with a bit of work, you can find a way to connect with pretty much anyone. (A little cheat sheet from before, remember to have empathy.)

5-MINUTE QUICK FIX

Think about someone that you do not really know but would like to get to know better. In what ways could you reach out and include them?

_____

_____

_____

_____

_____

_____

_____

_____

_____

_____

_____

_____

_____

_____

_____

_____

_____

_____

_____

5-MINUTE QUICK FIX

What does it mean to be inclusive? How does it feel when you are included in activities or conversations?

_____

_____

_____

_____

_____

_____

_____

_____

_____

_____

_____

_____

_____

_____

_____

_____

_____

_____

I AM WORTHY

10-MINUTE RESET

Carefully read each phrase three times out loud. Slowly repeat it as you inhale and exhale. Try looking in the mirror as you tell yourself these things!

"People want me around."

"I love making people feel important."

"It makes me happy to feel included."

"I am wanted, and I want people around me."

"I accept myself for who I am."

"I can be friends with anyone."

"No one is better than me, and I am not better than anyone."

"I'm happy to include people in activities."

10-MINUTE RESET

Write about the last time you felt abandoned or ignored. What happened? What led up to those feelings? Could you have done anything differently to change the outcome?

_____

_____

_____

_____

_____

_____

_____

_____

_____

_____

_____

_____

_____

_____

_____

_____

_____

_____

_____

_____

I AM WORTHY

15-MINUTE REGROUP

What are some things that you can do right now to help build friendships? (i.e., smile, ask questions, be interested in the other person's life).

_____

_____

_____

_____

_____

_____

_____

_____

_____

_____

_____

_____

_____

_____

_____

_____

_____

_____

_____

15-MINUTE REGROUP

List 3 qualities or characteristics that you possess that make you a good friend. Then, list 3 qualities and characteristics that you would want in a friend.

_____

_____

_____

_____

_____

_____

_____

_____

_____

_____

_____

_____

_____

_____

_____

_____

_____

_____

_____

_____

_____

_____

I AM WORTHY

30-MINUTE DEEP-DIVE

Make a list of the types of activities or situations *that you would like to be included in.* Then, jot down some of the people with whom you would like to do those activities.

_____

_____

_____

_____

_____

_____

_____

_____

_____

_____

_____

_____

_____

_____

_____

_____

_____

_____

_____

_____

_____

_____

30-MINUTE DEEP-DIVE

Make a list of the types of activities or situations *that you would like to invite people to join*. Then, jot down some of the people with whom you would like to do those activities.

_____

_____

_____

_____

_____

_____

_____

_____

_____

_____

_____

_____

_____

_____

_____

_____

_____

_____

_____

_____

I AM WORTHY

"Develop enough courage so that you can stand up for yourself and then stand up for somebody else."

— *Maya Angelou, American memoirist*

DEFEND

It's in our nature to defend ourselves, our stuff, and our loved ones. When you feel attacked or provoked, you might feel increased anxiety and anger. Enter the bullies. No one deserves to be bullied, but somehow bullies seem to keep showing up at the worst times.

Standing up for yourself sometimes is hard, especially if you feel alone. It's important to find people who care about you and will defend you — and people who know they can count on you to do the same. When you are constantly criticized for your actions, you might start to believe that something is wrong with being yourself. However, working towards feeling comfortable around people and not taking anything they say personally will help you realize the stuff that comes out of their mouths is most likely a reflection of how they see themselves. It's likely they lack self-esteem and gratitude, and it manifests in outbursts toward other people. Assert yourself. Ignore them. And stick with people that make you feel safe and loved.

I AM WORTHY

5-MINUTE QUICK FIX

Describe a time when you felt uncomfortable with how someone was talking to you or treating you. What were they saying, and how were they acting?

_____

_____

_____

_____

_____

_____

_____

_____

_____

_____

_____

_____

_____

_____

_____

_____

_____

5-MINUTE QUICK FIX

List 5 things you can do the next time you or one of your friends is being made fun of or criticized.

_____

_____

_____

_____

_____

_____

_____

_____

_____

_____

_____

_____

_____

_____

_____

_____

_____

_____

_____

I AM WORTHY

10-MINUTE RESET

Make a list of the negative things you think people think about you.
Next to each item, write down why that thing isn't true. Then, think
about what you can do to prevent yourself from believing each lie.

_____

_____

_____

_____

_____

_____

_____

_____

_____

_____

_____

_____

_____

_____

_____

_____

_____

_____

_____

10-MINUTE RESET

Describe the last time you witnessed someone getting bullied. What happened? Could you have done anything? How did each person react?

_____

_____

_____

_____

_____

_____

_____

_____

_____

_____

_____

_____

_____

_____

_____

_____

_____

_____

_____

_____

I AM WORTHY

15-MINUTE REGROUP

Reflect on a situation in which you felt attacked or needed to defend yourself. How did this make you feel? How could you handle the situation differently now?

_____

_____

_____

_____

_____

_____

_____

_____

_____

_____

_____

_____

_____

_____

_____

_____

_____

_____

_____

15-MINUTE REGROUP

Repeat the following affirmations. Then, draw a doodle for each one!

"I don't take comments personally."

"I don't allow other people's words to control how I feel about myself."

"I am my own cheerleader."

"I will step in if my friends or family need me to."

"If I see bullying, I will stop it."

"My friends can count on me."

"I am assertive."

"I deserve kindness."

"I am kind."

I AM WORTHY

30-MINUTE DEEP-DIVE

Think of the people you've seen treat others unkindly. List as many instances as you can think of. What happened? Write about why you think they treat people that way. Did anyone step in? What could have been done to change the outcome?

_____

_____

_____

_____

_____

_____

_____

_____

_____

_____

_____

_____

_____

_____

_____

_____

_____

_____

_____

30-MINUTE DEEP-DIVE

Put on music that inspires you. Describe characters in books or movies that you admire because they stood up for what they believe in. What were they fighting for? Who were they fighting? How did they prevail?

_____

_____

_____

_____

_____

_____

_____

_____

_____

_____

_____

_____

_____

_____

_____

_____

_____

_____

I AM WORTHY

"You and only you are responsible for your life choices and decisions."

— *Robert Kiyosaki, American entrepreneur*

EVALUATE

"Think before you act!" "Look before you leap!" You hear this all the time, but it's actually excellent advice. It may seem unexciting to assess your actions before you carry them out, but chances are, you'll save yourself from making quick decisions that might hurt you or others. (Like that snarky post you whipped out last week about your partner in Chem class.)

Before you react, respond, or join in — spend a moment thinking about what the next few days look like after you act. Will you say something to a friend you might regret tomorrow? Will someone overhear you whispering something that is hurtful to someone else? Could you be putting yourself in danger by tagging along? What seems like a good idea now may have consequences that cause pain and anxiety for you after the fact.

Friend, let's spend some time thinking about what it means to evaluate your decisions so you know how much of a risk you are willing to take if things go unexpectedly. Decisions you make now can affect you for many years later, even into adulthood, so having a strategy to help you evaluate before you act is always a good plan.

I AM WORTHY

5-MINUTE QUICK FIX

List 5 of your actions in the past that ended up causing you to be more anxious and worried after the fact. Did you know the possible outcome before you acted? If so, what made you do it anyway?

_____

_____

_____

_____

_____

_____

_____

_____

_____

_____

_____

_____

_____

_____

_____

_____

_____

_____

5-MINUTE QUICK FIX

What are 5 things you want to do but don't do? What prevents you from doing what you want?

_____

_____

_____

_____

_____

_____

_____

_____

_____

_____

_____

_____

_____

_____

_____

_____

_____

I AM WORTHY

10-MINUTE RESET

Describe the last time you had to accept the consequences of your actions. What was the situation, and how did it make you feel? Could you have changed the outcome? How so? If you could relive the moment, would you make a different decision?

_____

_____

_____

_____

_____

_____

_____

_____

_____

_____

_____

_____

_____

_____

_____

_____

_____

_____

_____

10-MINUTE RESET

Carefully read each phrase three times out loud. Slowly repeat it as you inhale and exhale. Try looking in the mirror as you tell yourself these things!

"I think before I act."

"My parents trust me to make careful decisions."

"My friends trust me to make careful decisions."

"I think about how what I say could make people feel."

"I count to 5 before responding to something that angers me."

"I don't listen to peer pressure."

"I don't have to prove myself to be popular."

"I act with kindness."

I AM WORTHY

15-MINUTE REGROUP

Imagine a friend came to you and wanted you to do something that made you feel uncomfortable. Make a list of risks you're not willing to take.

_____

_____

_____

_____

_____

_____

_____

_____

_____

_____

_____

_____

_____

_____

_____

_____

_____

_____

_____

15-MINUTE REGROUP

Research the phrase: Hindsight is 20/20. What does that mean, and what can you learn from that phrase?

_____

_____

_____

_____

_____

_____

_____

_____

_____

_____

_____

_____

_____

_____

_____

_____

_____

_____

I AM WORTHY

30-MINUTE DEEP-DIVE

Think of someone in your life that is dealing with negative consequences from a decision they made. What happened? What could have prevented the situation from happening? How has their life changed after the fact?

_____

_____

_____

_____

_____

_____

_____

_____

_____

_____

_____

_____

_____

_____

_____

_____

_____

_____

_____

_____

30-MINUTE DEEP-DIVE

What is something that you are currently trying to evaluate? Imagine two situations: One in which you decide to act and one in which you decide not to act. Create a pros and cons list for each scenario. Once done, circle the outcomes that might cause anxiety or worry. Draw a square around the outcomes that would make you very happy. Shade the outcomes that might have long-lasting effects. Do any overlap?

_____

_____

_____

_____

_____

_____

_____

_____

_____

_____

_____

_____

_____

_____

_____

_____

_____

_____

I AM WORTHY

CHAPTER 4: I AM PERFECT

Chances are you've been told through advertisements and your social media feed what the "perfect" life looks like. And, if what you see in the mirror doesn't match what you see on the screen, you might think you are wrong or flawed. There could be nothing further from the truth. Low self-esteem is a pervasive problem for many teenagers and even adults. When all you see in the mirror are flaws, it can greatly affect how you think about yourself and others. Mindful journaling can help you love and appreciate yourself as you are, in your already-perfect form. Let's sing it in our best singing voices... "You are beautiful just the way you are." (Thank you, Bruno Mars!)

In this chapter, we'll practice these five values, which can lead to a more confident and accepting outlook about your whole self.

Love: Learning to love yourself is a skill you'll need for your whole life. Learning to talk to yourself with respect and love might make you less anxious overall.

Discover: Spend time uncovering what makes you different and unique. A world full of people who are exactly alike makes for a boring world.

Accept: Although you likely have things about yourself that you would like to change (in a healthy way, of course), learning to accept yourself as you are now will help you meet your goals faster and more confidently.

Protect: Part of loving yourself is taking care of your body and mind so that you feel your best.

Forgive: When you hit slumps, forgive yourself and move on. Having standards that are difficult to maintain can cause unnecessary anxiety.

Exploring these values can help you love who you see in the mirror every time you look in one. Talk to yourself like you would a dear friend — you might find yourself feeling happier and healthier.

"You can't hate yourself happy. You can't criticize yourself thin. You can't shame yourself worthy. Real change begins with self-love and self-care."

— *Jessica Ortner, American author*

LOVE

Want a new best friend? Look in the mirror!! When you learn how to consistently love and appreciate yourself, it can ease some worries and anxieties. There is no such thing as a perfect body, appearance, or way to act, but it's hard not to compare yourself to what you see daily in your feed. By loving yourself and feeling comfortable and safe in your own skin, your self-doubt will likely start to fade.

Say positive things to yourself. Compliment your body in the mirror. Find things to love about every aspect of you. You are perfect just the way you are, and no matter what mistakes you've made or what you look like, you are a beautiful human being. Friend, love who you are now all the way into becoming and growing into who you will be in the future, and NEVER STOP LOVING YOU!

I AM PERFECT

5-MINUTE QUICK FIX

Write down a quick list of your favorite things about you. Why do you love these things?

_____

_____

_____

_____

_____

_____

_____

_____

_____

_____

_____

_____

_____

_____

_____

_____

_____

5-MINUTE QUICK FIX

Write a quick list of your least favorite things about yourself. How would you change them? And why do you want to?

_____

_____

_____

_____

_____

_____

_____

_____

_____

_____

_____

_____

_____

_____

_____

_____

_____

_____

_____

_____

I AM PERFECT

10-MINUTE RESET

Describe a situation where you felt self-conscious about how you looked or acted. Why do you think you felt that way? What could you do in the future to help avoid feeling the way you did?

_____

_____

_____

_____

_____

_____

_____

_____

_____

_____

_____

_____

_____

_____

_____

_____

_____

10-MINUTE RESET

Repeat the following affirmations. Then, draw a doodle for each one!

"I love and respect my body."

"I am beautiful and perfect just the way I am."

"I don't have to look or be a certain way to be loved."

"I have so much love for myself that I will never feel inadequate or unworthy of love."

"I have the strength to be confident just as I am."

"My soul knows that I am beautiful and strong."

"I love myself!"

"There is no perfect body other than the one I have."

I AM PERFECT

15-MINUTE REGROUP

What does self-love look like? Write 10 statements that describe what it means to love yourself, your personality, and your body.

_____

_____

_____

_____

_____

_____

_____

_____

_____

_____

_____

_____

_____

_____

_____

_____

_____

_____

_____

15-MINUTE REGROUP

What does self-criticism look like? Write 10 statements that describe what it means to be critical of yourself, your personality, and your body.

_____

_____

_____

_____

_____

_____

_____

_____

_____

_____

_____

_____

_____

_____

_____

_____

_____

_____

_____

_____

_____

_____

I AM PERFECT

30-MINUTE DEEP-DIVE

Has anyone ever made fun of you or a friend/family member because of how you/they acted or looked? What happened? If this had happened to a dear friend, what would you say to them to make them feel better?

_____

_____

_____

_____

_____

_____

_____

_____

_____

_____

_____

_____

_____

_____

_____

_____

_____

_____

_____

_____

_____

30-MINUTE DEEP-DIVE

List all of the things that make you uncomfortable about your appearance or personality. Next to each item, answer three questions:

1. Why do I feel uncomfortable about this aspect of myself?

2. What is amazing about this aspect of me that I might be overlooking?

3. Is this something that can be improved in a healthy way? If yes, how?

_____

_____

_____

_____

_____

_____

_____

_____

_____

_____

_____

_____

_____

_____

_____

_____

_____

_____

_____

I AM PERFECT

"Surround yourself with good people. People who are going to be honest with you and look out for your best interests."

— *Derek Jeter, Former professional baseball player*

DISCOVER

Friends, do you know you? Do you know where your ideas come from? If you have negative feelings about yourself, then find better role models. We often learn about how we are supposed to look and act from movies, TV, and social media.

Spending time discovering where your negative feelings come from can help determine if those influences are necessary in your life. (Newsflash: They aren't. Unfollow people who make you feel bad about yourself.)

Aim to fill your life with people who do and say interesting things, share real stories, uplift people, and help those in need. People who constantly talk about or show their life as pristine and "perfect" will no doubt cause you to think that you need to look like that, too. And that's just not real or healthy.

Dare to unfollow content and people that make you feel like your life is less perfect because it doesn't look like theirs.

I AM PERFECT

5-MINUTE QUICK FIX

List 5 social media accounts that you follow that make you feel good
about yourself.

_____

_____

_____

_____

_____

_____

_____

_____

_____

_____

_____

_____

_____

_____

_____

_____

_____

5-MINUTE QUICK FIX

List 5 social media accounts that you follow that can make you feel
negative thoughts about yourself. Could you unfollow them today?

_____

_____

_____

_____

_____

_____

_____

_____

_____

_____

_____

_____

_____

_____

_____

_____

_____

_____

_____

_____

_____

I AM PERFECT

10-MINUTE RESET

Carefully read each phrase three times out loud. Slowly repeat it as you inhale and exhale. Try looking in the mirror as you tell yourself these things!

"I am open to learning new things."

"There is more than one way to feel like a beautiful human being."

"The more open I am to new experiences, the happier I can be."

"I won't pretend to know everything; I will be open-minded."

"I will surround myself with uplifting people."

"I will find role models who care about more than appearance."

"I am not my appearance. I am my actions."

"I will always aim to be my authentic self."

10-MINUTE RESET

Describe a time when you were watching television or scrolling social media, and you felt bad about yourself afterward. What did you see? Can you pinpoint why you felt negative feelings?

_____

_____

_____

_____

_____

_____

_____

_____

_____

_____

_____

_____

_____

_____

_____

_____

_____

_____

_____

I AM PERFECT

15-MINUTE REGROUP

Look in the mirror and study your face and body. Discover new ways to describe your features that put them in a positive light. Example: Instead of "My ears are too big," say, "I'm proud to have my family member's ears." Do that for all of your features. Rewrite how you talk to yourself.

_____

_____

_____

_____

_____

_____

_____

_____

_____

_____

_____

_____

_____

_____

_____

_____

_____

_____

15-MINUTE REGROUP

What would it look like if your online presence could be anything you imagined without fear of being scrutinized by friends or family? Do you have any interests now that you hide from your online or in-person personality?

_____

_____

_____

_____

_____

_____

_____

_____

_____

_____

_____

_____

_____

_____

_____

_____

_____

_____

_____

_____

I AM PERFECT

30-MINUTE DEEP-DIVE

Where do you spend the majority of your time socializing? Online? At school? At home? Think about all your interactions throughout your day and describe the ones that make you feel happy and cared for. Then, write down the interactions that make you feel intimidated or self-conscious.

_____

_____

_____

_____

_____

_____

_____

_____

_____

_____

_____

_____

_____

_____

_____

_____

_____

_____

_____

30-MINUTE DEEP-DIVE

Turn on some music — music that really makes you happy! Then, go through all of your social media accounts and unfollow the accounts that potentially cause you to have anxious or negative thoughts. You are under no obligation to follow or be anyone's friend. If you don't want to unfollow, at least snooze them, so you don't see every post. Also, consider turning off your notifications for your social apps to reduce distractions throughout your day. You'll love the freedom!

_____

_____

_____

_____

_____

_____

_____

_____

_____

_____

_____

_____

_____

_____

_____

_____

_____

_____

I AM PERFECT

"Accepting yourself is about respecting yourself. It's about honoring yourself right now, here, in this moment. Not just who you could become somewhere down the line."

— *Kris Carr, American author and wellness activist*

ACCEPT

Friend, there is only one of you. If you can accept and love yourself AS YOU ARE in this moment, you could boost your self-esteem. This is not to say that you don't have things you want to change about yourself — everyone does — but you'll likely want to change because it will make you FEEL better, not because you want to be liked or impress others.

Accepting your whole self is also a way of accepting everyone around you. When you see everyone around you as equal and beautiful, it is easier to accept your own beauty and uniqueness. There's only one of you in this world. And what a lucky world that is!

5-MINUTE QUICK FIX

Identify six attributes that you really like about yourself.

_____

_____

_____

_____

_____

_____

_____

_____

_____

_____

_____

_____

_____

_____

_____

_____

_____

_____

5-MINUTE QUICK FIX

Think of a time when you felt comfortable in your own skin. Recall the emotions and feelings you felt at that moment.

_____

_____

_____

_____

_____

_____

_____

_____

_____

_____

_____

_____

_____

_____

_____

_____

_____

_____

_____

_____

_____

I AM PERFECT

10-MINUTE RESET

What are some steps you can take towards healthy self-acceptance?

_____

_____

_____

_____

_____

_____

_____

_____

_____

_____

_____

_____

_____

_____

_____

_____

_____

_____

10-MINUTE RESET

What does it mean to fully accept yourself as you are? When was the last time this happened for you?

_____

_____

_____

_____

_____

_____

_____

_____

_____

_____

_____

_____

_____

_____

_____

_____

_____

_____

I AM PERFECT

15-MINUTE REGROUP

Repeat the following affirmations. Then, draw a doodle for each one!

"I accept myself for exactly who I am."

"I am happy to be me!"

"I am grateful for everything I see in the mirror."

"I will not speak negatively about myself."

"I can love myself and try to improve myself at the same time."

15-MINUTE REGROUP

Write down everything you wish you could change about yourself. Now pretend this list belongs to your friend. Next to each item, write a supportive message to encourage your friend to celebrate and accept what's listed.

_____

_____

_____

_____

_____

_____

_____

_____

_____

_____

_____

_____

_____

_____

_____

_____

_____

_____

_____

_____

I AM PERFECT

30-MINUTE DEEP-DIVE

Write a love letter to yourself. What do you love most and why? How can you show yourself appreciation and gratitude every day?

_____

_____

_____

_____

_____

_____

_____

_____

_____

_____

_____

_____

_____

_____

_____

_____

_____

_____

_____

_____

_____

30-MINUTE DEEP-DIVE

Describe the last time you just accepted something the way it was. What were your expectations, and how did the outcome differ? What led to you accepting the outcome without worrying or feeling bad? How could this situation be adapted to other times this might happen in another area of your life?

_____

_____

_____

_____

_____

_____

_____

_____

_____

_____

_____

_____

_____

_____

_____

_____

_____

_____

_____

I AM PERFECT

"Positive thinking will let you do everything better than negative thinking."

— *Zig Ziglar, American author + motivational speaker*

PROTECT

When you're feeling good about yourself, it seems like it just takes one person to bring you down with their negative energy.

Friend, let's learn skills to guard your feelings when others use silence, judgment, or intimidation to make you feel small. There are ways to calm yourself and stay positive when you are in a situation that makes you feel scared, uncomfortable, or not good enough.

Mindful journaling, having a positive attitude, getting enough exercise and sleep, and having positive people in your life are just some ways to protect yourself from life's difficult times...and people. :)

I AM PERFECT

5-MINUTE QUICK FIX

List your five favorite active activities. What type of exercise do you like the most?

_____

_____

_____

_____

_____

_____

_____

_____

_____

_____

_____

_____

_____

_____

_____

_____

_____

_____

5-MINUTE QUICK FIX

Take a moment to focus on your breath. Slow down and breathe in and out. Imagine what it looks like if you are committed to taking care of your body and your mind. Write down what you visualized.

_____

_____

_____

_____

_____

_____

_____

_____

_____

_____

_____

_____

_____

_____

_____

_____

_____

_____

_____

_____

I AM PERFECT

10-MINUTE RESET

What is your usual bedtime and wake-up time? Do you feel like you are getting enough sleep? Is there anything about your night and morning routine you'd like to change?

_____

_____

_____

_____

_____

_____

_____

_____

_____

_____

_____

_____

_____

_____

_____

_____

_____

_____

10-MINUTE RESET

Carefully read each phrase three times out loud. Slowly repeat it as you inhale and exhale. Try looking in the mirror as you tell yourself these things!

"I am committed to taking good care of myself."

"I will protect my heart and body."

"I am not going to let hateful words make me feel bad about myself."

"I will take care of myself by controlling how I react to situations."

"It's important for me to take care of my body by getting sleep, exercising, and eating healthy."

"I will treat myself with kindness."

"I will do things that are good for my body and mind."

I AM PERFECT

15-MINUTE REGROUP

Think about someone in your life who is really good at taking care of their mind, body, and soul. How do they do it? What are their consistent actions? What can you learn from them? If you don't know, ask them.

_____

_____

_____

_____

_____

_____

_____

_____

_____

_____

_____

_____

_____

_____

_____

_____

15-MINUTE REGROUP

Write down 10 ways you can take better care of yourself. Next to each one, make a plan for how you can incorporate it into your current schedule.

_____

_____

_____

_____

_____

_____

_____

_____

_____

_____

_____

_____

_____

_____

_____

_____

_____

_____

_____

_____

_____

I AM PERFECT

30-MINUTE DEEP-DIVE

Let's imagine a perfect day. From the time you wake up until the time you go to sleep, describe everything that happens and how in those moments, you are fully dedicated to treating yourself in the best way possible. (What does your morning look like? What do you eat for lunch? How do your social interactions play out?)

_____

_____

_____

_____

_____

_____

_____

_____

_____

_____

_____

_____

_____

_____

_____

_____

_____

_____

_____

_____

30-MINUTE DEEP-DIVE

Grab your calendar or schedule for next week. Find times within the next week that you can schedule time for mental or physical care.

_____
_____
_____
_____
_____
_____
_____
_____
_____
_____
_____
_____
_____
_____
_____
_____
_____
_____
_____
_____
_____
_____
_____

I AM PERFECT

"Forgiving yourself, believing in yourself, and choosing to love yourself are the best gifts one could receive."

— *Brittany Burgunder, Certified professional life coach*

FORGIVE

Friend, can you think about that recurring thought in the back of your mind where you play out the same scenario, wishing you could have changed the outcome? You likely did something you're not proud of, and you can't stop beating yourself up about it. Our brains love a good drama! It's like — get over it, BRAIN, that was a year ago! If this is happening to you, there's a good chance you haven't forgiven yourself for that moment. It's not easy to forgive and move on — it's almost easier to keep punishing yourself.

But, when you finally forgive yourself, you learn an important lesson: forgiveness can reduce anxious thoughts and increase your self-esteem. Let's work on learning how to forgive ourselves and move on!

5-MINUTE QUICK FIX

Write about what it means to forgive. Is it easy for you to forgive others? Yourself?

_____

_____

_____

_____

_____

_____

_____

_____

_____

_____

_____

_____

_____

_____

_____

_____

_____

5-MINUTE QUICK FIX

How does forgiving yourself help you in the future?

_____

_____

_____

_____

_____

_____

_____

_____

_____

_____

_____

_____

_____

_____

_____

_____

_____

_____

_____

_____

_____

I AM PERFECT

10-MINUTE RESET

Write about the last time you forgave someone. What happened, and why did they ask for your forgiveness?

_____

_____

_____

_____

_____

_____

_____

_____

_____

_____

_____

_____

_____

_____

_____

_____

_____

_____

10-MINUTE RESET

Write three ways that forgiving someone else has helped you.

_____

_____

_____

_____

_____

_____

_____

_____

_____

_____

_____

_____

_____

_____

_____

_____

_____

_____

_____

_____

I AM PERFECT

15-MINUTE REGROUP

Make a list of everything you beat yourself up about. Next to each item, write down what it would take to forgive yourself and move on.

_____

_____

_____

_____

_____

_____

_____

_____

_____

_____

_____

_____

_____

_____

_____

_____

_____

_____

_____

15-MINUTE REGROUP

Repeat the following affirmations. Then, draw a doodle for each one!

"People make mistakes and deserve forgiveness."

"I am not perfect, and it's okay to make mistakes."

"I am a forgiving person."

"It's important to forgive people when they make mistakes."

"Forgiving others helps me to forgive myself."

"Forgiveness is important for my self-esteem."

I AM PERFECT

30-MINUTE DEEP-DIVE

Write yourself a letter to forgive yourself for any mistakes you've made or ways you've punished yourself in the past.

_____

_____

_____

_____

_____

_____

_____

_____

_____

_____

_____

_____

_____

_____

_____

_____

_____

30-MINUTE DEEP-DIVE

Write a letter to someone who you've struggled to forgive.

_____

_____

_____

_____

_____

_____

_____

_____

_____

_____

_____

_____

_____

_____

_____

_____

_____

_____

_____

_____

_____

I AM PERFECT

CONCLUSION

Okay, Friend! How do you feel? If you're at this point, you've really put this journal to use! Mindfulness is a practice that can benefit how you feel at home, in the classroom, with your friends and when you look in the mirror. When you are able to make journaling a part of your life, it can help you manage stress, develop healthy habits and cope with the ups and downs of your teen life. You are loved, intelligent, worthy, and above all — *perfect just as you are*.

ADDITIONAL PUBLICATIONS

The Mindfulness Workbook for Teen Girls — *coming Summer 2023*

Daily Gratitude Journal — *coming Summer 2023*

PAPER MOUNTAIN
PUBLISHING

ABOUT PAPER MOUNTAIN PUBLISHING

Our mission at Paper Mountain Publishing, LLC is to ignite an enduring love for reading and self-improvement. We are committed to producing excellent children, young adult, and adult books, creating captivating narratives and insightful resources that foster change and contribute to a balanced well-being.

Through our uplifting publications, we offer empowering learning opportunities for all ages. Our books, guided by mindfulness and respect for the present, serve as guiding lights in life's many stages. We recognize the transformative power of words and their capacity to inspire growth and wisdom.

Made in the USA
Las Vegas, NV
29 November 2024

12927425R00125